Like T

Dona Herweck Rice

Publishing Credits

Rachelle Cracchiolo, M.S.Ed., *Publisher*
Conni Medina, M.A.Ed., *Managing Editor*
Nika Fabienke, Ed.D., *Content Director*
Véronique Bos, *Creative Director*
Shaun N. Bernadou, *Art Director*
Carol Huey-Gatewood, M.A.Ed., *Editor*
John Leach, *Assistant Editor*
Courtney Roberson, *Senior Graphic Designer*

Image Credits: All images from iStock and/or Shutterstock.

Teacher Created Materials
5301 Oceanus Drive
Huntington Beach, CA 92649-1030
www.tcmpub.com
ISBN 978-1-4938-9859-6
© 2019 Teacher Created Materials, Inc.
Printed in China
Nordica.082018.CA21800936

 like her.

Stand

 like him.

Stand

2

 **so you can**

Stand

be like them.

 like her.

Wink

 like him.

Wink

Wink

so you can

be like them.

 like her.

Walk

 like him.

Walk

 **so you can**

Walk

be like them.

 like her.

Hop

 like him.

Hop

Hop

so you can

be like them.

 like her.

Kick

 like him.

Kick

Kick

so you can

be like them.

High-Frequency Words

New Words

can	her
him	like
so	them

Review Words

be	you